CHAFFLES

© **Copyright 2019 by Zara Elby All rights reserved.**

This document is geared towards providing exact and reliable information in regards to the topic and issue covered. The publication is sold with the idea that the publisher is not required to render accounting, officially permitted, or otherwise, qualified services. If advice is necessary, legal or professional, a practiced individual in the profession should be ordered.

- From a Declaration of Principles which was accepted and approved equally by a Committee of the American Bar Association and a Committee of Publishers and Associations.

In no way is it legal to reproduce, duplicate, or transmit any part of this document in either electronic means or in printed format. Recording of this publication is strictly prohibited and any storage of this document is not allowed unless with written permission from the publisher. All rights reserved.

The information provided herein is stated to be truthful and consistent, in that any liability, in terms of inattention or otherwise, by any usage or abuse of any policies, processes, or directions contained within is the solitary and utter responsibility of the recipient reader. Under no circumstances will any legal responsibility or blame be held against the publisher for any reparation, damages, or monetary loss due to the information herein, either directly or indirectly.

Respective authors own all copyrights not held by the publisher.

The information herein is offered for informational purposes solely, and is universal as so. The presentation of the information is without contract or any type of guarantee assurance.

TABLE OF CONTENTS

Introduction 1
CHAPTER 1: Understanding the Keto Diet 2
CHAPTER 2: What are Chaffles? 5
CHAPTER 3: Recipes 7
Conclusion 66

INTRODUCTION

This book contains an introduction to the ketogenic diet but more importantly, it will teach you simple chaffle recipes you can make at home, which will help you along your keto journey.

The ketogenic diet—a low-carb, high-fat diet—has grown in popularity among health experts, fitness coaches, bodybuilders, and just about anyone who wants lose weight. Although starting a new diet can be intimidating, there are recipes out there that can make things a lot more manageable.

Specifically, this book introduces chaffles, a waffle made from egg and cheese. These two ingredients are keto-friendly, and it only takes a maximum of five minutes to cook a chaffle with a conventional waffle maker.

The chaffle is an especially versatile type of food. In fact, you can customize it to suit your tastes. This book contains dozens of chaffle recipes that are all keto-friendly, easy to make, and come in sweet and savory versions. There's always a chaffle recipe for any occasion.

Thanks for downloading this book, and I hope these recipes will help make your ketogenic journey a little more manageable and stress-free.

CHAPTER 1:
UNDERSTANDING THE KETO DIET

People who want to lose weight can exercise all they want and not get the results they desire unless they make significant changes to their diet. This is where the 70-30 rules come in—70% diet and 30% exercise.

The ketogenic diet is essentially a diet that limits carbohydrate intake but puts emphasis fat consumption. It is defined similarly to other low-carb diets like the Atkins diet, but has a few specific characteristics of its own.

This chapter briefly summarizes the ketogenic diet, how it works, and its benefits.

HOW THE KETOGENIC DIET WORKS

Essentially, the ketogenic diet works by drastically reducing carbohydrate intake while simultaneously increasing fat intake. This gradually leads your body into ketosis—a metabolic state where the body starts burning fats instead of carbohydrates for energy. Fat gets converted into ketones in the liver, and supplies energy for the muscles and brain. At the same time, it helps reduce blood sugar and insulin resistance.

KETOGENIC DIET HEALTH BENEFITS

When done properly, most diets provide benefits to a person's health. The ketogenic diet provides the following benefits:
1. It's great for people with diabetes and for those who are still in the prediabetes stage.
2. It reduces the risk of Alzheimer's disease, Parkinson's, and other age-related diseases.
3. It supplies energy for the brain and can prevents seizures.
4. It improves a person's mental alertness.
5. It's a great for women diagnosed with polycystic ovarian syndrome (PCOS).

There are different types of ketogenic diets and these differ depending on the end goal desired.

The first one is the standard ketogenic diet (SKD) which is composed of low-carb, moderate protein, and high-fat foods. It's comprised of 75% fat, 20% protein, and only 5% carbs. This is the most researched and most frequently recommended by nutritionists and health experts.

Another type is the high-protein ketogenic diet, which is comprised of 60% fat, 35% protein, and 5% carbs. As the name suggests, it's suited to people who need more protein in their diet.

The cyclical ketogenic diet (CKD) has higher carb refeeds, in which five days of standard ketogenic diet should be followed by two days of high carbohydrate intake.

The targeted ketogenic diet (TKD) adds more carbs around workouts. Due to variations in the diet setup, CKD and TKD target the more advanced dieters, particularly bodybuilders and athletes.

RECOMMENDED FOODS TO INCLUDE IN THE KETO DIET

Since the ketogenic diet is a low-carb, high-fat type of diet, you'll have to include foods that are high in fat content, particularly in mono- and polyunsaturated fats. Examples of foods that do great in ketogenic diets are meat, fatty fish, butter, cream, eggs, nuts, seeds, low-carb vegetables, avocados, and healthy oils.

To better plan out your ketogenic meals, it's often helpful to look at sample meal plans online. If you feel overwhelmed with all the different recipes, you might want to focus on easy recipes that won't require too many ingredients, nor will require you to spend too much time preparing.

A great example of a recipe that would go well with breakfast, lunch, and dinner are chaffles. The next chapters will walk you through understanding what a chaffle is, and how you can easily make your own using different variations.

CHAPTER 2:
WHAT ARE CHAFFLES?

When running a search for ketogenic food recipes, you'll find images and recipes of chaffles. "But they look like waffles," you think. You might be confused as to how a piece of bread made it to the ketogenic diet, but chaffles are more than what they appear to be.

A chaffle is a low-carb food that looks just like a waffle. However, instead of flour and sugar, it's made of egg and grated cheese beaten together (hence the name "chaffle" — cheese + waffle). The batter is then cooked in, as you've probably guessed, a waffle maker. It makes for a perfect breakfast fix and can be batch-made to reserve for future meals.

A BRIEF HISTORY

The first chaffles weren't low-carb at all and consisted of churros and waffles. It seemed to have originated from the kitchen of a vegan taco restaurant called Seabirds Kitchen in Southern California. These chaffles were coated with cinnamon sugar and topped with vegan ice cream. They also came in a variety of sweet syrups that aren't keto-friendly. Since then, different versions of chaffles came out from countries like Japan and Iran.

The keto-friendly chaffle started from the Instagram account of a trainer and meal planner specializing in keto. Today, there are over 8,000 posts related to chaffles not only on Instagram but all over the Internet.

HOW TO MAKE CHAFFLES

To make a basic chaffle, using one large egg is enough, and the cheese should be shredded to help it melt easily. The egg and cheese are whisked together, and the batter transferred onto a heated waffle maker. Cook it for 2-3 minutes, or leave it for another 1-2 minutes to make the surface extra crispy.

The cheese should be able to melt easily but still maintain some structure. For this, you can use either cheddar or mozzarella.

You can also add almond flour for a more bread-like texture and to help cut down the taste of egg. Seasonings and toppings can also be added, even avocado for that extra flavor.

For the waffle maker, you can either use a mini waffle maker, or you can use a larger one if you want to make more in one go.

To serve, chaffles can come in special sauces that are sugar-free. There's the Choc Zero Maple Syrup, which sticky and thick like traditional syrup. There's also the Lakanto Maple Syrup, which isn't as thick as Choc Zero but tastes just as great.

Due to their simplicity in composition, chaffles can come in different versions—basic, savory, sweet, and cake-like. If you'd like to include chaffles in your daily keto meal plan, the next chapter compiles recipes of different types of chaffles for you to try out.

CHAPTER 3:
RECIPES

Before you try out these recipes, make sure the equipment and tools you'll be using are ready. You might want to have the following in your kitchen:

- A whisk or a fork for mixing, or a blender with a whisk attachment
- A waffle maker, or mini waffle maker
- A bowl for mixing in the ingredients

That's basically it! Now on to the recipes!

BASIC WAFFLES

Serves: 2

Nutritional Information (per serving):
Calories: 170 | Carbohydrates: 2g | Fat: 6g | Protein: 10g

INGREDIENTS:

- 1 egg
- 1/2 cup cheddar cheese, shredded
- 1 tbsp almond flour

DIRECTIONS:

1. Preheat a mini waffle maker.
2. Mix egg and cheddar cheese in a small mixing bowl. Stir until both ingredients are blended well.
3. Add the almond flour.
4. Pour half the batter onto the heated waffle maker.
5. Allow the batter to cook for 3-4 minutes. Leave on for another 1-2 minutes if you want it crispy.
6. Repeat.

CINNAMON CHAFFLES

Serves: 1

Nutritional Information (per serving):
Calories: 150 | Carbohydrates: 6.5g | Fat: 9g | Protein: 10.7g

INGREDIENTS:

- 1 egg
- 1 cup mozzarella cheese
- 1 shake of cinnamon powder
- 1 tsp vanilla extract
- 1 tbsp almond flour
- 1 tsp baking powder
- Spray oil

DIRECTIONS:

1. Mix egg and vanilla extract in a bowl.
2. Add the almond flour, baking powder, and cinnamon.
3. Add mozzarella cheese to the mixture.
4. Preheat the waffle maker and spray some oil on it.
5. Add half of the batter into the waffle maker. Cook for 5 minutes or until golden and crispy.
6. Add the remaining batter and cook for another 5 minutes.

PIZZA CHAFFLE

Serves: 1

Nutritional Information (per serving):
Calories: 76 | Carbohydrates: 4.1g | Fat: 4.3g | Protein: 5.5g

INGREDIENTS:

- 1 egg
- 1/2 cup mozzarella cheese, shredded
- A pinch of Italian seasoning
- 1 tbsp pizza sauce
- Pepperoni and more cheese, for topping

DIRECTIONS:

1. Preheat a mini waffle maker.
2. Whisk seasonings and eggs together in a small bowl.
3. Sprinkle half the shredded cheese onto the waffle maker. Cook for 30 seconds until crispy.
4. Add half the batter and let it cook for 4 minutes until golden and crispy.
5. Remove the cooked chaffle. Pour in the remaining batter.
6. Pour pizza sauce onto cooked chaffles and spread until the top is well-covered.
7. Add shredded cheese and pepperoni for toppings.

MAPLE PUMPKIN CHAFFLE

Serves: 2

Nutritional Information (per serving):
Calories: 201 | Carbohydrates: 4g | Fat: 15g | Protein: 12g

INGREDIENTS:

- 2 eggs
- 3/4 tsp baking powder
- 2 tsp 100% pumpkin puree
- 3/4 tsp pumpkin pie spice
- 4 tsp heavy whipping cream
- 2 tsp sugar-free maple syrup
- 1 tsp coconut flour
- 1/2 cup mozzarella cheese, shredded
- 1/2 tsp vanilla
- Pinch of salt

DIRECTIONS:

1. Preheat the waffle maker.
2. Combine all ingredients in a small mixing bowl.
3. If you're using a mini waffle maker, pour around 1/4 of the batter. Allow to cook for 3-4 minutes.
4. Repeat.

BLUEBERRY CHAFFLE

Serves: 1

Nutritional Information (per serving):
Calories: 116 | Carbohydrates: 3g | Fat: 8g | Protein: 8g

INGREDIENTS:

- 2 eggs
- 1 cup mozzarella cheese
- 2 tbsp almond flour
- 1 tsp baking powder
- 1 tsp cinnamon
- 2 tsp confectioner's sugar
- 3 tbsp blueberries
- Spray oil

DIRECTIONS:

1. Preheat a mini waffle maker and spray with oil.
2. Add all the remaining ingredients in a mixing blow. Mix until well-combined.
3. Add around 1/4 cup of blueberries to your batter.
4. Pour in the batter onto the waffle maker. Allow to cook for 3-5 minutes until crispy and golden.

NUTTY CHAFFLES

Serves: 1

Nutritional Information (per serving):
Calories: 66.5 | Carbohydrates: 3g | Fat: 4.5g | Protein: 7.2g

INGREDIENTS:

- 1 egg
- 1 tsp coconut flour
- 1 1/2 tbsp unsweetened cocoa
- 2 tbsp sugar-free sweetener
- 1 tbsp heavy cream
- 1/2 tsp baking powder
- 1/2 tsp vanilla

DIRECTIONS:

1. Preheat the waffle maker.
2. Combine all the ingredients in a small bowl. Mix well.
3. Pour half the batter into the waffle maker. Allow to cook for 3-5 minutes until golden brown and crispy.
4. Carefully remove and add the remaining batter.

CRISPY CHAFFLE WITH EVERYTHING BUT THE BAGEL SEASONING

Serves: 1

Nutritional Information (per serving):
Calories: 287 | Carbohydrates: 6g | Fat: 20g | Protein: 21g

INGREDIENTS:

- 2 eggs
- 1/2 cup parmesan cheese
- 1 tsp everything but the bagel seasoning
- 1/2 cup mozzarella cheese
- 2 tsp almond flour

DIRECTIONS:

1. Preheat the waffle maker.
2. Sprinkle the mozzarella cheese onto the waffle maker. Let it melt and cook for 30 seconds until crispy. Remove this from the waffle maker.
3. Using a whisk, combine eggs, parmesan, almond flour, seasoning, and the toasted cheese in a small bowl.
4. Pour the batter into the waffle maker.
5. Allow the batter to cook for 3-4 minutes until crispy and golden brown in color.

STRAWBERRY AND CREAM CHEESE LOW-CARB KETO WAFFLES

Serves: 2

Nutritional Information (per serving):
Calories: 86 | Carbohydrates: 2.4g | Fat: 8.3g | Protein: 5g

INGREDIENTS:

- 2 tsp coconut flour
- 4 tsp monkfruit
- 1/4 tsp baking powder
- 1 egg
- 1 oz cream cheese, softened
- 1/2 tsp vanilla extract
- 1/4 cup strawberries

DIRECTIONS:

1. Preheat the waffle maker.
2. In a bowl put in the coconut flour, then add the baking powder and the monkfruit.
3. Add in the egg, cream cheese, and vanilla extract. Mix well with a whisk.
4. Pour the batter into the preheated waffle maker and allow to cook for 3-4 minutes.
5. Allow chaffles to cool before topping with strawberries.

GARLIC BREAD CHAFFLES

Serves: 1

Nutritional Information (per serving):
Calories: 74 | Carbohydrates: 0.9g | Fat: 6.5g | Protein: 3.4g

INGREDIENTS:

- 1 egg
- 1/2 cup mozzarella cheese, grated
- 2 tbsp almond flour
- 1/2 tsp garlic powder
- 1/2 tsp oregano
- 1/2 tsp salt
- Olive oil, for greasing

For the topping:

- 2 tbsp butter, unsalted and softened
- 1/2 tsp garlic powder
- 1/4 cup mozzarella cheese, grated

DIRECTIONS:

1. Preheat the waffle maker. Lightly grease it with olive oil.
2. Beat the egg in a mixing bowl.
3. Add in the almond flour, mozzarella, garlic powder, salt, and oregano. Mix well.
4. Use a spoon and place the first batch of batter into the center, then gently spread it towards the edges.
5. Close the lid. Let the batter cook for up to 5 minutes.
6. Use a pair of tongs to take out the cooked chaffle.
7. Cut the chaffle into 4 strips.
8. Preheat your grill and place the chaffle sticks on a tray.
9. Mix the garlic powder with butter and spread on top of the sticks.
10. Sprinkle a bit of mozzarella over the sticks and place inside the grill. Allow to cook for 2-3 minutes until the cheese melts and bubbles.

CHICKEN PARMESAN CHAFFLE

Serves: 1

Nutritional Information (per serving):
Calories: 125 | Carbohydrates: 2.6g | Fat: 8.3g | Protein: 9.4g

INGREDIENTS:

- 1/2 cup chicken breast, shredded
- 1/4 cup cheddar cheese
- 1/6 cup parmesan cheese
- 1 egg
- 1 tsp Italian seasoning
- 1/8 tsp garlic powder
- 1 tsp cream cheese, room temperature

For the toppings:

- 2 slices provolone cheese
- 1 tbsp sugar-free pizza sauce

DIRECTIONS:

1. Preheat the waffle maker.
2. Add 1 tsp of shredded cheese to the preheated waffle maker and wait for 3 seconds before taking it out. The cheese should be toasted.
3. Add the remaining ingredients, except toppings, in a medium-sized mixing bowl. Mix well.
4. Mix the toasted cheese with the chaffle batter.
5. Pour batter onto the waffle maker and allow to cook for 4-5 minutes until crispy and golden brown in color.
6. Repeat these steps for the remaining batter to make a second chaffle.
7. Allow chaffles to cool before topping with the sugar-free pizza sauce and provolone cheese.

CHEESY GARLIC CHAFFLE

Serves: 1

Nutritional Information (per serving):
Calories: 141 | Carbohydrates: 2.6g | Fat: 9g | Protein: 12.6g

INGREDIENTS:

- 1 egg
- 1/2 cup mozzarella cheese, shredded
- 1 tsp Italian seasoning
- 1/2 tsp garlic powder
- 1 tsp cream cheese

For the topping:

- 1 tbsp butter
- 1/2 tsp Italian seasoning
- 1/2 tsp garlic powder
- 2 tbsp mozzarella cheese, shredded
- Parsley or Italian seasoning

DIRECTIONS:

1. Preheat a waffle maker and preheat the oven to 350 degrees F.
2. Mix all the garlic bread chaffle ingredients in a small mixing bowl.
3. Divide the batter in half. Cook the first half in the waffle maker for at least 4 minutes. You can add shredded cheese first and allow to cook for 30 seconds before adding in the batter for that toasty, cheesy crust.
4. After cooking the garlic bread chaffles, place them in a lined baking tray.
5. Place butter in a small bowl. Put it in the microwave for a maximum of 10 seconds.
6. Add the garlic to the melted butter.

7. Use a small basting brush to apply the butter mixture to the chaffles.
8. Sprinkle mozzarella cheese on top. You may also sprinkle Italian seasoning if desired.
9. Bake the chaffles for 5 minutes, or until you see the cheese toppings melt.
10. Serve with marinara sauce if desired.

CORNBREAD CHAFFLE

Serves: 1

Nutritional Information (per serving):
Calories: 150 | Carbohydrate: 1.1g | Fat: 11.8g | Protein: 9.6g

INGREDIENTS:

- 1 egg
- 1/2 cup cheddar cheese, shredded
- 5 jalapeno slices
- 1 tsp hot sauce
- 1/4 tsp corn extract
- Salt

DIRECTIONS:

1. Preheat the waffle maker for 30 seconds.
2. While preheating, start whipping the egg in a small bowl.
3. Throw in the other ingredients until you make a batter.
4. Cook a teaspoon of cheese on the waffle maker for 30 seconds. Add this to the batter afterwards.
5. Pour half the batter onto the waffle maker.
6. Allow the batter to cook for 3-5 minutes.
7. Remove cooked chaffles. Allow to cool before digging in.

STUFFING WITH CHAFFLE

Serves: 1

Nutritional Information (per serving):
Calories: 229 | Carbohydrates: 4.6g | Fat 17.6g | Protein: 13.7g

INGREDIENTS:

- 2 eggs
- 1/2 cup mozzarella, cheddar, or a combination of both, shredded
- 1/4 tsp garlic powder
- 1/2 tsp onion powder
- 1/2 tsp dried poultry seasoning
- 1/4 tsp salt
- 1/4 tsp pepper

For the stuffing:

- 1 onion, small and diced
- 2 celery stalks
- 4 oz mushrooms, diced
- 4 tbsp butter
- 3 eggs

DIRECTIONS:

1. Preheat the waffle maker.
2. Preheat your oven to 350 degrees F.
3. Combine the ingredients for the chaffle in a small bowl. Mix well.
4. Pour 1/4 of the chaffle batter into the waffle maker. Cook for up to 4 minutes. Continue making chaffles until you've used up all the batter. Set aside.
5. Sauté celery, mushrooms, and onions on a small frying pan.
6. Tear up the chaffles into small pieces and combine with the sautéed vegetables and eggs in a separate bowl. Mix well.
7. Place the stuffing mixture into a small casserole dish. Put it in the oven. Bake for around 30-40 minutes.

BIRTHDAY CAKE CHAFFLE

Serves: 1

Nutritional Information (per serving):
Calories: 141 | Carbohydrate: 4.7g | Fat: 10.2g | Protein: 4.7g

INGREDIENTS:

- 2 eggs
- 1/4 cup almond flour
- 1 tsp coconut flour
- 2 tbsp butter, melted
- 2 tbsp cream cheese, room temperature
- 1 tsp cake batter extract
- 1/2 tsp vanilla extract
- 1/2 tsp baking powder
- 2 tbsp monkfruit
- 1/4 tsp xanthan powder

For the frosting:

- 1/2 cup heavy whipping cream
- 2 tbsp monkfruit
- 1/2 tsp vanilla extract

DIRECTIONS:

1. Preheat the waffle maker.
2. Blend all chaffle ingredients in a blender until the consistency is creamy and smooth. Allow the batter to sit for 1 minute.
3. Add 2-3 tbsp of the batter into the preheated waffle maker. Allow to cook for 2-3 minutes.
4. Mix frosting ingredients in a separate bowl. Use a hand mixer until peaks start to form.
5. Cool the chaffles first before adding the frosting.

PUMPKIN CHAFFLE WITH CREAM CHEESE GLAZE

Serves: 1

Nutritional Information (per serving):
Calories: 84 | Carbohydrate: 5.3g | Fat: 4.5g | Protein: 6.1g

INGREDIENTS:

- 1 egg
- 1/2 cup mozzarella cheese
- 1/2 tsp pumpkin pie spice
- 1 tbsp pumpkin

For the cream cheese frosting:

- 2 tbsp cream cheese, softened at room temperature
- 2 tbsp monkfruit
- 1/2 tsp vanilla extract

DIRECTIONS:

1. Preheat the waffle maker.
2. Whip the egg in a small bowl.
3. Add cheese, pumpkin, and pumpkin pie spice to the whipped egg and mix well.
4. Add half the batter to the waffle maker and allow to cook for 3-4 minutes.
5. While waiting for the chaffle to cook, combine all the ingredients for the frosting in another bowl. Continue mixing until a smooth and creamy consistency is reached. Feel free to add more butter if you prefer a more buttery taste.
6. Allow the chaffle to cool before frosting it with cream cheese.

BANANA NUT CHAFFLES

Serves: 1

Nutritional Information (per serving):
Calories: 119 | Carbohydrate: 2.7g | Fat: 7.8g | Protein: 8.8g

INGREDIENTS:

- 1 egg
- 1 tbsp cream cheese, softened at room temperature
- 1/2 cup mozzarella cheese
- 1 tbsp monkfruit
- 1/4 tsp vanilla extract
- 1/4 tsp banana extract

For optional toppings:

- Caramel sauce, sugar-free
- Pecans or other nuts

DIRECTIONS:

1. Preheat the mini waffle maker.
2. Whip the egg in a small mixing bowl.
3. Throw in the other ingredients and whisk together until everything is well-combined.
4. Divide the mixture into 2. Pour the first half onto the waffle maker and cook for 4-5 minutes until golden brown. Remove cooked chaffle and repeat for the remaining batter.
5. Serve with sauces.

RED VELVET CHAFFLES

Serves: 1

Nutritional Information (per serving):
Calories: 74 | Carbohydrate: 3.8g | Fat: 5.8g | Protein: 4.4g
(Note that the values above are for the chaffles only)

INGREDIENTS:

For the chaffle:

- 2 tbsp monkfruit
- 1 tbsp dutch processed cocoa
- 1 egg
- 2 drops red food coloring, optional
- 1/4 tsp baking powder
- 1 tbsp whipping cream

For the frosting:

- 2 tbsp monkfruit
- 2 tbsp cream cheese, softened at room temperature
- 1/4 tsp vanilla extract

DIRECTIONS:

1. Preheat the waffle maker.
2. As the waffle maker is heating, whip the egg in a small bowl.
3. Add in the remaining chaffle ingredients. Continue mixing until you achieve a creamy and smooth consistency.
4. Pour 1/2 of the batter into the waffle maker and allow to cook for 2-3 minutes. Take out the cooked chaffle and pour in the remaining batter to make a second chaffle.
5. Mix the sweetener, vanilla, and cream cheese in a separate bowl.
6. Allow the chaffles to cool before frosting.

LEMON CHAFFLES

Serves: 1

Nutritional Information (per serving):
Calories: 221 | Carbohydrate: 5.2g | Fat: 20.3 | Protein: 5.6g

INGREDIENTS:

- 2 eggs
- 2 oz cream cheese, softened at room temperature
- 2 tsp butter, melted
- 2 tbsp coconut flour
- 1 tsp monkfruit
- 1 tsp baking powder
- 1/2 tsp lemon extract
- 20 drops cake batter extract

For the frosting:

- 1/2 cup heavy whipping cream
- 1 tbsp monkfruit
- 1/4 tsp lemon extract

DIRECTIONS:

1. Preheat the waffle maker.
2. Add all chaffle ingredients in a blender. Blend until the consistency is creamy.
3. Scoop up some batter. Place the batter onto the preheated waffle maker. If you're using a mini waffle maker, one scoop of batter is the perfect amount for one chaffle.
4. Cook chaffles for 3-4 minutes.
5. While the chaffles are cooking, combine the frosting ingredients in a separate bowl. Mix until soft peaks start to form.
6. Transfer cooked chaffles and allow to cool before frosting.
7. Grate lemon peel and sprinkle over the frosted chaffles for extra flavor.

PEANUT BUTTER CAKE CHAFFLE

Serves: 1

Nutritional Information (per serving):
Calories: 92 | Carbohydrate: 3.6g | Fat: 7g | Protein: 5.5g

INGREDIENTS:

- 1 egg
- 2 tbsp peanut butter powder, sugar-free
- 1/4 tsp baking powder
- 2 tbsp monkfruit
- 1 tbsp cream cheese, softened
- 1/4 tsp peanut butter extract (optional)

For the frosting:

- 1 tbsp butter, softened
- 2 tbsp monkfruit
- 2 tbsp cream cheese, softened
- 1/4 tsp vanilla extract

DIRECTIONS:

1. Preheat the waffle maker.
2. Use a whisk to whip up the egg in a small bowl.
3. Once the egg is whipped, put in the remaining ingredients and mix until you form a smooth and creamy batter.
4. Divide the batter into two halves. Put the first half in the preheated waffle maker. Allow this to cook for 2-3 minutes.
5. Repeat for the remaining batter.
6. To make the frosting, add the cream cheese, peanut butter, sweetener, and vanilla to a separate bowl and mix well.
7. Spread frosting onto cooled chaffles.
8. If you prefer glaze, heat the frosting and drizzle over the chaffles.

CHURRO CHAFFLE

Serves: 1

Nutritional Information (per serving):
Calories: 76 | Carbohydrate: 4.1g | Fat: 4.3g | Protein: 5.5g

INGREDIENTS:

- 1 egg
- 1/2 cup mozzarella cheese, shredded
- 2 tbsp swerve brown sweetener
- 1/2 tsp cinnamon

DIRECTIONS:

1. Preheat the mini waffle maker.
2. Start whipping the egg in a small bowl. If you don't have a whisk, you can use a fork.
3. Combine shredded cheese with the whipped eggs.
4. Place 1/2 of the mixture onto the waffle maker. Cook this for 4 minutes or until the color becomes golden brown.
5. While you wait for the chaffles to cook, begin mixing cinnamon and sweetener in another bowl.
6. Once the chaffles are cooked, cut them into strips and add to the sweet cinnamon mixture. Don't wait until they go cold because chaffles soak up more moisture while still hot.

CHOCOLATE CAKE CHAFFLE

Serves: 1

Nutritional Information (per serving):
Calories: 37 | Carbohydrate: 2g | Fat: 2.9g | Protein: 2.2g
(Does not include the frosting)

INGREDIENTS:

- 2 tbsp cocoa
- 1 egg
- 2 tbsp monkfruit
- 1 tbsp heavy whipping cream

For the frosting:

- 2 tbsp monkfruit
- 2 tbsp cream cheese, softened
- 1/4 tsp vanilla

DIRECTIONS:

1. Preheat the waffle maker.
2. Whip the egg in a small mixing bowl.
3. Once you've whipped the egg, add in the remaining ingredients except for the frosting ingredients.
4. Divide the mixture into two and pour the first half onto the waffle maker. Allow to cook for 2-3 minutes.
5. While waiting, mix vanilla, cream cheese, and sweetener in another bowl. Mix until these three ingredients are well combined.
6. Spread the frosting once your chaffles have cooled to room temperature.

CHAFFLE TWINKIES

Serves: 6

Nutritional Information (per serving):
Calories: 100 | Carbohydrate: 4g | Fat: 6g | Protein: 4g

INGREDIENTS:

- 2 eggs
- 2 oz cream cheese, softened
- 2 tbsp butter, melted
- 1 tsp vanilla extract
- 1/2 tsp vanilla cupcake extract, optional
- 1/4 cup lakanto
- A pinch of pink salt
- 1/4 cup almond flour
- 2 tbsp coconut flour
- 1 tsp baking powder

DIRECTIONS:

1. Preheat the waffle maker.
2. Melt butter and let it cool.
3. In a small bowl, whisk the butter and eggs together until it becomes creamy.
4. Add in the salt, vanilla extract, and sweetener.
5. Add the baking powder, coconut flour, and almond flour.
6. Mix all ingredients to form a batter.
7. Add around 2 tbsp of the batter into the waffle maker. Spread evenly.
8. Close the lid. Allow the batter cook for up to 4 minutes.
9. Remove the cooked chaffles and let it cool.

BACON CHEDDAR BAY BISCUITS CHAFFLE

Serves: 1

Nutritional Information (per serving):
Calories: 185 | Carbohydrate: 4.3g | Fat: 12.5g | Protein: 7.7g

INGREDIENTS:

- 1/2 cup almond flour
- 1/cup at fiber
- 3 strips bacon, cooked to a crisp and crumbled
- 1 egg, beaten
- 1/4 cup sour cream
- 1 tbsp bacon grease, melted
- 1 1/2 tbsp butter, melted
- 1/2 cup cheddar cheese, shredded
- 1/2 cup smoked gouda cheese, shredded
- 1/4 tsp swerve confectioners
- 1/2 tsp garlic salt
- 1/2 tsp onion powder
- 1/2 tsp parsley, dried
- 1/2 tsp baking powder
- 1/4 tsp baking soda

DIRECTIONS:

1. Preheat the waffle maker.
2. While waiting for it to heat up, mix baking powder, baking soda, almond flour, onion powder, and garlic salt in a bowl.
3. In a separate mixing bowl, combine bacon, bacon grease, eggs, parsley, sour cream, cheese, and melted butter.
4. After mixing, pour the dry ingredients in the bowl with the wet ingredients and mix well.
5. Scoop up 2-3 tbsp of the mixture and place it on the preheated waffle maker. Allow this to cook for 5-6 minutes. Repeat the steps until the entire mixture has been cooked.

CRUNCH CEREAL CAKE CHAFFLE

Serves: 1

Nutritional Information (per serving):
Calories: 154 | Carbohydrate: 5.6g | Fat: 11.2g | Protein: 4.6g
(Does not include the toppings)

INGREDIENTS:

For the chaffles:

- 1 egg
- 2 tbsp almond flour
- 1/2 tsp coconut flour
- 1 tbsp butter, melted
- 1 tbsp cream cheese, softened
- 1/4 tsp vanilla extract
- 1/4 tsp baking powder
- 1 tbsp confectioners sweetener
- 1/8 tsp xanthan gum

For the toppings:

- 20 drops captain cereal flavoring
- Whipped cream

DIRECTIONS:

1. Preheat the mini waffle maker.
2. Blend or mix all the chaffles ingredients until the consistency is creamy and smooth. Allow to rest for a few minutes so that the flour absorbs the liquid ingredients.
3. Scoop out 2-3 tbsp of batter and put it into the waffle maker. Allow to cook for 2-3 minutes.
4. Top the cooked chaffles with freshly whipped cream.
5. Add syrup and drops of Captain Cereal flavoring for a great flavor.

BAKED POTATO CHAFFLE USING JICAMA

Serves: 1

Nutritional Information (per serving):
Calories: 168 | Carbohydrates: 5.1g | Fat: 11.8g | Protein: 10g

INGREDIENTS:

- 1 jicama root
- 1/2 onion, medium, minced
- 2 cloves garlic, pressed
- 1 cup cheese
- 1 eggs, whisked
- Salt and pepper

DIRECTIONS:

1. Peel the jicama root and shred it using a food processor.
2. Place the shredded jicama root in a colander to allow the water to drain. Mix in 2 tsp of salt as well.
3. Squeeze out the remaining liquid.
4. Microwave the shredded jicama for 5-8 minutes. This step pre-cooks it.
5. Mix all the remaining ingredients together with the jicama.
6. Start preheating the waffle maker.
7. Once preheated, sprinkle a bit of cheese on the waffle maker, allowing it to toast for a few seconds.
8. Place 3 tbsp of the jicama mixture onto the waffle maker. Sprinkle more cheese on top before closing the lid.
9. Cook for 5 minutes. Flip the chaffle and let it cook for 2 more minutes.
10. Serve your baked jicama by topping it with sour cream, cheese, bacon pieces, and chives.

FRIED PICKLE CHAFFLE STICKS

Serves: 1

Nutritional Information (per serving):
Calories: 465 | Carbohydrate: 3.3g | Fat: 22.7g | Protein: 59.2g

INGREDIENTS:

- 1 egg
- 1/2 cup mozzarella cheese
- 1/4 cup pork panko
- 6-8 pickle slices, thinly sliced
- 1 tbsp pickle juice

DIRECTIONS:

1. Mix all the ingredients, except the pickle slices, in a small bowl.
2. Use a paper towel to blot out excess liquid from the pickle slices.
3. Add a thin layer of the mixture to a preheated waffle iron.
4. Add some pickle slices before adding another thin layer of the mixture.
5. Close the waffle maker's lid and allow the mixture to cook for 4 minutes.

Optional: Combine hot sauce with ranch to create a great-tasting dip.

TIRAMISU CHAFFLE

Serves: 8

Nutritional Information (per serving):
Calories: 567 | Carbohydrate: 6.6g | Fat: 53.4g | Protein: 14.7g

INGREDIENTS:

- 2 eggs
- 2 oz cream cheese, softened
- 1 tbsp coconut flour
- 1 tbsp heavy cream
- 1 tsp vanilla extract
- 1/2 tsp baking powder
- 1/2 tsp ground cinnamon
- 1/4 tsp stevia powder

For the coffee syrup:

- 4 tbsp strong coffee
- 5 drops liquid stevia

For the filling:

- 1 oz cream cheese, softened
- 3 oz mascarpone cheese, softened
- 1/4 cup heavy cream
- 2 tsp vanilla extract
- 1/4 tsp stevia powder

For dusting:

- 1/2 tsp unsweetened cocoa powder

DIRECTIONS:

1. Preheat the mini waffle maker.
2. Combine all the chaffle ingredients in a blender.
3. Once the waffle maker is heated, pour about 1/4 of the batter and allow it to cook for 5-6 minutes. Remove the cooked chaffle and repeat this step for the remaining batter.

4. While waiting for the chaffle to cook, mix the liquid stevia and coffee in a small bowl for the coffee syrup.
5. For the filling, mix the vanilla, stevia powder, and heavy cream. Whisk this until soft peaks start to form.
6. In a separate mixing bowl, use a hand mixer to combine the mascarpone and cream cheese. Once done, mix it in with the whipped cream.
7. To assemble, drizzle 1 tbsp of coffee syrup on the chaffle.
8. On one chaffle, spread a quarter of the filling. Top this with another chaffle, and repeat the previous step until you have four layers of chaffles.
9. Dust the finished tiramisu chaffle with the unsweetened cocoa powder.
10. Refrigerate this for 6 hours or more before serving.

SPICY JALAPENO POPPER CHAFFLES

Serves: 1

Nutritional Information (per serving):
Calories: 231 | Carbohydrate: 2g | Fat: 18g | Protein: 13g

INGREDIENTS:

For the chaffles:

- 1 egg
- 1 oz cream cheese, softened
- 1 cup cheddar cheese, shredded

For the toppings:

- 2 tbsp bacon bits
- 1/2 tbsp jalapenos

DIRECTIONS:

1. Turn on the waffle maker. Preheat for up to 5 minutes.
2. Mix the chaffle ingredients.
3. Pour the batter onto the waffle maker.
4. Cook the batter for 3-4 minutes until it's brown and crispy.
5. Remove the chaffle and repeat steps until all remaining batter have been used up.
6. Sprinkle bacon bits and a few jalapeno slices as toppings.

BREAKFAST CHAFFLE SANDWICH

Serves: 1

Nutritional Information (per serving):
Calories: 514 | Carbohydrates: 2g | Fat: 47g | Protein: 21g

INGREDIENTS:

- 1 egg
- 1/2 cup monterey jack cheese
- 1 tbsp almond flour
- 2 tbsp butter

DIRECTIONS:

1. Preheat the waffle maker for 5 minutes until it's hot.
2. Combine Monterey Jack cheese, almond flour, and the egg in a bowl. Mix well.
3. Take 1/2 of the batter and pour it into the preheated waffle maker. Allow to cook for 3-4 minutes.
4. Repeat previous step for the remaining batter.
5. Melt butter on a small pan. Just like you would with French toast, add the chaffles and let each side cook for 2 minutes. To make them crispier, press down on the chaffles while they cook.
6. Remove the chaffles from the pan. Allow to cool for a few minutes. Serve.

BLT CHAFFLE

Serves: 1

Nutritional Information (per serving):
Calories: 699 | Carbohydrates: 5g | Fat: 65g | Protein: 20g

INGREDIENTS:

- 1 egg
- 4 cheese slices, thinly sliced
- 3 bacon slices, cooked
- 1 lettuce leaf
- 2 slices tomato
- 2 tbsp mayonnaise
- Cooking spray

DIRECTIONS:

1. Crack and whip the egg inside a measuring cup.
2. Turn on the waffle maker and grease with cooking spray.
3. Allow the waffle maker to heat up.
4. Cut the corners off the two slices of cheese. You may omit this step but it helps the cheese to fit better inside a mini waffle maker.
5. Place the cheese on the hot waffle maker and let it melt.
6. When the cheese melts, pour the whipped eggs over it.
7. Add another slice of cheese over the egg.
8. Close the waffle maker lid and allow the mixture to cook for 3 minutes.
9. Carefully remove the cooked chaffle and repeat previous steps until all mixture is used up.
10. Add bacon, tomato, lettuce, and mayonnaise to the first chaffle.
11. Add mayonnaise on the second chaffle and assemble your keto chaffle BLT.

PEANUT BUTTER AND JELLY CHAFFLES

Serves: 1

Nutritional Information (per serving):
Calories: 337 | Carbohydrates: 3g | Fat: 27g | Protein: 21g

INGREDIENTS:

- 1 egg
- 2 slices cheese, thinly sliced
- 1 tsp natural peanut butter
- 1 tsp sugar-free raspberry preserve
- Cooking spray

DIRECTIONS:

1. Crack and whisk the egg in a small bowl or a measuring cup.
2. Lightly grease the waffle maker with cooking spray.
3. Preheat the waffle maker.
4. Once it is heated up, place a slice of cheese on the waffle maker and wait for it to melt.
5. Once melted, pour the egg mixture onto the melted cheese.
6. Once the egg starts cooking, carefully place another slice of cheese on the waffle maker.
7. Close the lid. Cook for 3-4 minutes.
8. Take out the chaffles and place on a plate.
9. Top the chaffles with whipped cream.
10. Drizzle some natural peanut butter and raspberry preserve on top.

HALLOUMI CHEESE CHAFFLES

Serves: 1

Nutritional Information (per serving):
Calories: 333 | Carbohydrates: 2g | Fat: 26g | Protein: 22g

INGREDIENTS:

- 3 oz halloumi cheese
- 2 tbsp pasta sauce

DIRECTIONS:

1. Make half-inch thick slices of halloumi cheese.
2. With the waffle maker still turned off, place the cheese slices on it.
3. Turn on the waffle maker and let the cheese cook for 3-6 minutes.
4. Remove from the waffle maker and let it cool.
5. Add low-carb pasta or marinara sauce.

CHOCOLATE CHIP CANNOLI CHAFFLES

Serves: 4

Nutritional Information (per serving):
Calories: 187 | Carbohydrates: 7g | Fat: 13g | Protein: 7g

INGREDIENTS:

For the chocolate chip chaffle:

- 1 tbsp butter, melted
- 1 tbsp monkfruit
- 1 egg yolk
- 1/8 tsp vanilla extract
- 3 tbsp almond flour
- 1/8 tsp baking powder
- 1 tbsp chocolate chips, sugar-free

For the cannoli topping:

- 2 oz cream cheese
- 2 tbsp low-carb confectioners sweetener
- 6 tbsp ricotta cheese, full fat
- 1/4 tsp vanilla extract
- 5 drops lemon extract

DIRECTIONS:

1. Preheat the mini waffle maker.
2. Mix all the ingredients for the chocolate chip chaffle in a mixing bowl. Combine well to make a batter.
3. Place half the batter on the waffle maker. Allow to cook for 3-4 minutes.
4. While waiting for the chaffles to cook, start making your cannoli topping by combining all ingredients until the consistency is creamy and smooth.
5. Place the cannoli topping on the cooked chaffles before serving.

CHAFFLES BENEDICT

Serves: 4

Nutritional Information (per serving):
Calories: 601 | Carbohydrates: 1g | Fat: 51g | Protein: 34g

INGREDIENTS:

For the chaffles:

- 12 eggs
- 1 cup cheddar cheese, shredded
- 8 slices bacon

For the Hollandaise sauce:

- 3 egg yolks
- 1 tbsp lemon juice
- 2 pinches kosher salt
- 1/4 tsp dijon mustard or hot sauce, optional
- 1/2 cup butter, salted

DIRECTIONS:

1. Preheat the waffle maker.
2. Pour water in a pan and place over medium-high heat.
3. Take 4 eggs and beat them in a bowl. The remaining eggs are for poaching.
4. Once the waffle maker is heated up, sprinkle 1 tbsp of cheese and allow it to toast.
5. Take 1 1/2 tbsp of the beaten eggs and place on the toasted cheese.
6. Once the egg starts cooking, add another layer of sprinkled cheese on top.
7. Close the lid. Cook for 2-3 minutes.
8. Remove the cooked chaffle and repeat the steps until you've created 8 chaffles.

9. Fry bacon and set aside for later.
10. Poach the remaining eggs.
11. To make the sauce, combine lemon juice, salt, egg yolks, and Dijon mustard or hot sauce in a bowl.
12. In a separate container, melt the butter in the microwave. Let it cool for a few minutes.
13. Pour the melted butter over the egg yolk mixture.
14. Using an immersion blender, pulse the mixture until it becomes yellow and cloudy. Continue pulsing until the consistency becomes creamy and thick.
15. To serve, place cooked chaffles on a plate.
16. Place a slice of bacon over each chaffle.
17. Top the bacon with poached egg and drizzle with hollandaise sauce.

CARNIVORE CHAFFLE

Serves: 1

Nutritional Information (per serving):
Calories: 274 | Carbohydrates: 1g | Fat: 20g | Protein: 23g

INGREDIENTS:

- 1 egg
- 1/3 cup mozzarella cheese
- 1/2 cup pork rinds
- Salt

DIRECTIONS:

1. Preheat the waffle maker.
2. In a small mixing bowl, mix a pinch of salt with the cheese, egg, and pork rinds.
3. Pour the mixture onto the preheated waffle maker. Close the lid and wait for 3-5 minutes while it cooks. You'll know it's cooked once it already has a golden brown color.
4. Carefully remove it from the waffle maker and serve.

EGGNOG CHAFFLES

Serves: 1

Nutritional Information (per serving):
Calories: 266 | Carbohydrates: 2g | Fat: 23g | Protein: 13g

INGREDIENTS:

- 1 egg, separated
- 1 egg yolk
- 1/2 cup mozzarella cheese, shredded
- 1/2 tsp spiced rum
- 1 tsp vanilla extract
- 1/4 tsp nutmeg, dried
- A dash of cinnamon
- 1 tsp coconut flour

For the icing:

- 2 tbsp cream cheese
- 1 tbsp powdered sweetener
- 2 tsp rum or rum extract

DIRECTIONS:

1. Preheat the mini waffle maker.
2. Mix egg yolk in a small bowl until smooth.
3. Add in the sweetener and mix until the powder is completely dissolved.
4. Add the coconut flour, cinnamon, and nutmeg. Mix well.
5. In another bowl, mix rum, egg white, and vanilla. Whisk until well combined.
6. Throw in the yolk mixture with the egg white mixture. You should be able to form a thin batter.
7. Add the mozzarella cheese and combine with the mixture.
8. Separate the batter into two batches. Put 1/2 of the batter into the waffle maker and let it cook for 6 minutes until it's solid.

9. Repeat until you've used up the remaining batter.
10. In a separate bowl, mix all the icing ingredients.
11. Top the cooked chaffles with the icing, or you can use this as a dip.

CHEDDAR JALAPENO CHAFFLES

Serves: 1

Nutritional Information (per serving):
Calories: 509 | Carbohydrates: 5g | Fat: 45g | Protein: 23g

INGREDIENTS:

- 1 egg
- 1/2 cup cheddar cheese, shredded
- 1 tbsp almond flour
- 1 tbsp jalapenos
- 1 tbsp olive oil

DIRECTIONS:

1. Preheat the waffle maker.
2. While waiting for the waffle maker to heat up, mix jalapeno, egg, cheese, and almond flour in a small mixing bowl.
3. Lightly grease the waffle maker with olive oil.
4. In the center of the waffle maker, carefully pour the chaffle batter. Spread the mixture evenly toward the edges.
5. Close the waffle maker lid and wait for 3-4 minutes for the mixture to cook. For an even crispier texture, wait for another 1-2 minutes.
6. Remove the chaffle. Let it cool before serving.

CREAM PUFF CHAFFLES

Serves: 4

Nutritional Information (per serving):
Calories: 390 | Carbohydrates: 3.2g | Fat: 37.7g | Protein: 9.1g

INGREDIENTS:

- 2 eggs
- 2 oz cream cheese, softened
- 1 tbsp coconut flour
- 1 tbsp heavy cream
- 1 tsp vanilla extract
- 1/2 tsp baking powder
- 1/4 tsp stevia powder
- 1/2 tsp ground cinnamon

For the custard filling:

- 4 egg yolks
- 1 tbsp stevia powder
- 1/4 tsp xanthan gum
- 1 cup heavy cream
- 1 tbsp vanilla extract

For dusting:

- 1/2 tsp confectioner's sweetener

DIRECTIONS:

1. Preheat the waffle maker.
2. Blend all the chaffle ingredients together.
3. Into the preheated waffle maker, pour about 1/4 of the batter.
4. Close the lid. Cook for 5-6 minutes.
5. Remove the cooked chaffle using a pair of tongs.
6. Repeat step 3 to cook the remaining batter.
7. Prepare the custard filling by whisking stevia and egg yolks. Add in the xanthan gum and combine well.

8. Place a saucepan over medium heat. Add in the heavy cream and bring to a simmer.
9. Add the heavy cream to the egg yolk mixture and whisk quickly.
10. Transfer the mixture onto the saucepan and continue stirring with a spatula or whisk. Continue whisking until the mixture thickens.
11. Turn off the heat. Continue to stir for 20 or 30 seconds.
12. Mix in the vanilla.
13. Using a fine mesh sieve, strain the custard cream. Place a cling wrap over it and refrigerate for an hour.
14. Take out the cold custard from the fridge. Remove the wrap and transfer to a bowl. Cut it using a whisk and place in a piping bag.
15. Using a knife, cut small pockets in each chaffle.
16. Begin piping the custard cream into the chaffle pockets.
17. Dust the chaffles with the powdered sweetener.

APPLE CINNAMON CHAFFLES

Serves: 1

Nutritional Information (per serving):
Calories: 185 | Carbohydrates: 7g | Fat: 10g | Protein: 12g

INGREDIENTS:

- 2 tbsp coconut flour
- 1 tsp baking powder
- 2 tsp cinnamon
- 1/2 tsp monkfruit sweetener
- 3 eggs
- 1/4 cup Granny smith apple, skinned and diced
- 3/4 cup mozzarella cheese, shredded
- 3/4 cup cheddar cheese, shredded
- Cooking spray

For the vanilla bean sauce:

- 1 egg yolk
- 2 oz cream cheese, softened
- Vanilla bean sauce
- 1/2 tsp monkfruit sweetener
- 1/2 tsp vanilla extract
- 1 cup whipping cream
- 1 tbsp butter
- Whole vanilla bean

DIRECTIONS:
1. Preheat the waffle maker.
2. Spray a low-carb non-stick spray on it to prevent the chaffles from sticking.
3. Make the chaffles by beating the eggs until it becomes frothy.
4. Add in the cheese and mix well.

5. In a separate bowl, whisk flour, cinnamon, sweetener, and baking powder.
6. Into the egg mixture, add the remaining dry ingredients. Mix well.
7. Add the diced apples, carefully folding them in.
8. Once more, spray the waffle maker with cooking spray before pouring batter into it.
9. Allow the batter to cook for 4 minutes until the surface turns brown.
10. Remove and allow the chaffle to cool.
11. Prepare the sauce by placing the butter, heavy whipping cream, and vanilla bean in a medium saucepan.
12. Heat the saucepan over medium heat. When the mixture starts to boil, add sweetener and adjust the heat to low. Simmer for another 10 minutes.
13. Take out the vanilla beans and discard. Scrape the remaining seeds into the whipping cream.
14. Remove the mixture from heat and whisk in the egg yolk.
15. Add the cream cheese and stir until it's melted.
16. Store the vanilla sauce in a container and leave in the fridge to cool.
17. Once the sauce has cooled, use this as topping for the chaffles.

CHICKEN CHAFFLE RECIPE

Serves: 1

Nutritional Information (per serving):
Calories: 508 | Carbohydrates: 7g | Fat: 40.7g | Protein: 29.3g

INGREDIENTS:

For the chicken:

- Coconut oil, for frying
- 1 lb chicken tenderloins, lightly flattened

For the marinade:

- 1 cup heavy whipping cream
- 2 tsp apple cider vinegar
- 2 tsp tabasco hot sauce
- 1/4 tsp ground black pepper
- 1 tsp sea salt

For the chicken coating:

- 1/2 cup almond flour
- 1/4 cup coconut flour
- 1/4 cup parmesan cheese, finely grated
- 1 tsp paprika
- 1/2 tsp onion powder
- 1/2 tsp garlic powder
- 1/4 tsp ground black pepper
- 1/4 tsp cayenne pepper
- 2 eggs, lightly beaten for use as egg wash

For the chaffles:

- 2 eggs
- 1 cup almond flour
- 1/4 cup coconut flour
- 2 tsp baking powder
- 1/2 cup mozzarella cheese, shredded

DIRECTIONS:

1. Start by preparing the chicken, rinse chicken and pat dry. Gently flatten with a mallet.
2. Mix together apple cider vinegar, hot sauce, heavy cream, salt, and pepper in a large bowl.
3. Mix in the chicken and marinade for at least 1 1/2 hours or overnight.
4. Prepare two bowls. In the first bowl, mix in all the dry ingredients. In the second bowl, whisk together the eggs. This will be your egg wash.
5. Dip the chicken in the egg wash before coating with the dry ingredients. Shake off excess coating.
6. Fry your chicken on medium-high heat. Cook until both sides are lightly brown.
7. Place chicken on a baking tray. Proceed to cover it with foil, and bake in the oven for 15-20 minutes at 350 degrees F.
8. Preheat the waffle maker.
9. Combine the chaffle ingredients in a bowl.
10. Place batter onto the preheated waffle maker and cook for 4-5 minutes until it's crispy and golden brown.
11. Remove chaffle. Serve alongside the chicken.

HOT BROWN SANDWICH CHAFFLE

Serves: 2

Nutritional Information (per serving):
Calories: 572 | Carbohydrates: 3g | Fat: 41g | Protein: 41g

INGREDIENTS:

For the chaffles:

- 1 egg, beaten
- 1/4 cup cheddar cheese, shredded and divided

For the sandwich:

- 2 slices fresh tomato
- 1/2 lb roasted turkey breast
- 1/2 tsp parmesan cheese, grated
- 2 bacon, cooked

For the sauce:

- 2 oz cream cheese, cubed
- 1/3 cup heavy cream
- 1/4 cup swiss cheese, shredded
- 1/4 tsp ground nutmeg
- White pepper

DIRECTIONS:

1. Preheat the waffle maker.
2. Start by making the chaffle, once heated up, sprinkle 1 tbsp cheddar cheese onto the iron.
3. After 30 seconds, top the cheese with beaten egg.
4. Once the egg starts to cook, top the mixture with another layer of cheese.
5. Close the waffle maker lid and allow to cook for 3-5 minutes until the chaffle is crispy and golden brown.

6. Take out the cooked chaffle and repeat the steps until you've used up all the batter.
7. Make the sauce by combining heavy cream and cream cheese in a small saucepan.
8. Place saucepan over medium heat and whisk until the cheese completely dissolves.
9. Add in Swiss cheese and parmesan, then continue whisking to melt the cheese.
10. Add in the white pepper and nutmeg.
11. Continue whisking until you achieve a smooth consistency.
12. Remove the sauce pan from heat.
13. Prepare the sandwich by setting the oven for broiling.
14. Cover a cookie sheet with aluminum foil.
15. Lightly grease the foil with butter, and place two chaffles on it.
16. Top the chaffles with 4 oz of turkey and a slice of tomato each. Add some sauce and grated parmesan on top.
17. Broil the chaffle sandwiches for 2-3 minutes until you see the sauce bubble and brown spots appear on top.
18. Remove from the oven. Put them on a heatproof plate.
19. Arrange bacon slices in a crisscross manner on top of the sandwich before serving.

BRULEED FRENCH TOAST CHAFFLE MONTE CRISTO

Serves: 1

Nutritional Information (per serving):
Calories: 368 | Carbohydrate: 7g | Fat: 22g | Protein: 34g

INGREDIENTS:

For the chaffles:

- 1 egg
- 1/8 tsp baking powder
- 1/4 tsp cinnamon
- 1/2 tsp monkfruit
- 1 tbsp cream cheese
- 2 tsp brown sugar substitute

For the filling:

- 2 oz deli ham
- 2 oz deli turkey
- 1 slice provolone cheese
- 1/2 tsp sugar-free jelly

DIRECTIONS:

1. Preheat the waffle maker.
2. Place all the chaffle ingredients, except the sugar substitute, inside a blender. Make sure to place the cream cheese closest to the blades. Blend the ingredients until you achieve a smooth consistency.
3. Sprinkle the waffle maker with 1/2 tsp of brown sugar substitute.
4. Onto the waffle maker, pour 1/2 of the batter. Sprinkle another 1/2 teaspoon of the brown sugar substitute.
5. Close the lid and allow the batter to cook for 3-5 minutes.
6. Remove the chaffle. Repeat the steps until you used up all the batter.

7. Prepare the chaffle by spreading jelly on one surface of the chaffle.
8. Following this order, place the ham, turkey, and cheese in a small, microwaveable bowl. Place inside the microwave. Heat until the cheese is melted.
9. Invert the bowl onto the chaffle so that the contents transfer onto the chaffle. The cheese should be under the ham and turkey, directly sitting on top of the chaffle.
10. Top with the other chaffle and flip it over before serving.

LEMON CHAFFLE DOME CAKE

Serves: 4

Nutritional Information (per serving):
Calories: 405 | Carbohydrates: 3g | Fat: 38g | Protein: 9g

INGREDIENTS:

For the chaffles:

- 2 eggs
- 2 oz cream cheese, softened
- 1 tbsp coconut flour
- 2 tsp heavy cream
- 2 tsp lemon juice
- 1/2 tsp vanilla extract
- 1/4 tsp stevia powder
- 1/4 tsp baking soda

For the lemon frosting:

- 8 oz cream cheese, softened
- 2 oz unsalted butter, softened
- 1 tbsp stevia powder
- 1 tbsp lemon zest
- 1 tsp lemon juice
- 1/2 tsp vanilla extract

DIRECTIONS:

1. Preheat the mini waffle maker.
2. Combine all the chaffle ingredients using a blender.
3. Onto the preheated waffle maker, pour 1/4 of the batter.
4. Close the lid. Let the batter cook for 4-5 minutes. Remove the cooked chaffle using a pair of silicone tongs.
5. Repeat the steps to use up the remaining batter.
6. Let the chaffles cool completely.
7. Make the lemon frosting by combining the ingredients in a bowl.
8. Assemble by cutting two of the chaffles in half.

9. Use cling wrap to line a small bowl.
10. Place a whole chaffle in the bowl, carefully molding it to the shape of the bowl.
11. Line each side with the four chaffle halves.
12. Add half the amount of lemon frosting.
13. Cover the frosting with the last whole chaffle.
14. Cover the bowl with cling wrap. Put in the fridge for 30 minutes. You don't need to chill the remaining lemon frosting.
15. Invert the chaffle dome onto a plate.
16. Spread the remaining lemon frosting over it. Add decorations if desired.
17. Chill the cake for another 30 minutes. Serve.

KEEMA CURRY CHAFFLE

Serves: 4

Nutritional Information (per serving):
Calories: 374 | Carbohydrate: 8g | Fat: 25g | Protein: 27g

INGREDIENTS:

For the chaffles:

- 2 eggs
- 3 oz mozzarella cheese, shredded
- 3 tbsp almond flour
- 1/2 tsp baking powder
- 1/4 tsp garlic powder

For the keema curry:

- 10.5 oz ground beef
- 1 tbsp avocado oil
- 1/4 tsp salt
- 1/2 tsp garlic powder
- 1/4 tsp ginger powder
- 1/2 cup tomato puree
- 2 tbsp curry powder
- 2 tbsp Worcestershire sauce

For the topping:

- 4 tsp parmesan cheese, finely grated

DIRECTIONS:

1. Start by making the curry, over medium heat, heat avocado oil in a frying pan.
2. Add in the ground meat and cook until it turns brown.
3. Add the ginger powder, garlic powder, and salt. Stir well.
4. Stir in the Worcestershire sauce and the tomato puree.
5. Finally, add the curry powder and stir it in.
6. Allow to simmer for about 6-10 minutes over low heat.
7. Preheat the mini waffle maker.

8. Combine all chaffle ingredients, except cheese, in a small mixing bowl.
9. Sprinkle some cheese onto the heated waffle maker and let it melt.
10. When the cheese melts, immediately pour 1/4 of the batter on top of it. Spread 2 tsp of keema curry then sprinkle some more cheese.
11. Close the lid. Cook for 4 minutes.
12. Remove the cooked chaffle and repeat the steps until you've used up all the batter.
13. Once all chaffles are cooked, use the remaining keema curry on top.
14. Top all the chaffles with parmesan cheese.

BROCCOLI AND CHEESE CHAFFLES

Serves: 1

Nutritional Information (per serving):
Calories: 170 | Carbohydrates: 2g | Fat: 13g | Protein: 11g

INGREDIENTS:

- 1 egg
- 1/2 cup cheddar cheese
- 1/4 cup broccoli, freshly chopped
- 1/4 tsp garlic powder
- 1 tbsp almond flour

DIRECTIONS:

1. Preheat the waffle maker.
2. In a mixing bowl, combine cheddar cheese, almond flour, garlic powder, and egg. If you don't have a whisk, you can use a fork.
3. Pour in the cheese batter and half the chopped broccoli in the waffle maker. Allow to cook for 4 minutes.
4. Let the chaffle cool for 1-2 minutes before serving.

CHEESE AND HOT HAM CHAFFLES

Serves: 1

Nutritional Information (per serving):
Calories: 435 | Carbohydrate: 4g | Fat: 32g | Protein: 31g

INGREDIENTS:

- 1 egg
- 1/2 cup Swiss cheese, shredded
- 1/4 cup Deli ham, chopped
- 1/4 tsp garlic salt
- 1 tbsp mayonnaise
- 2 tsp Dijon mustard

DIRECTIONS:

1. Preheat the waffle maker.
2. In a small bowl, start whisking the egg. Then add the ham, cheese, and garlic salt. Mix all the ingredients well.
3. Scoop up half of the batter and place in the hot waffle maker. Allow this to cook for 3-4 minutes.
4. Remove the cooked chaffle and repeat the previous step for the remaining batter.
5. For the dip, stir the Dijon mustard and mayonnaise together until full mixed.

Optional: You may slice the chaffles in halves, or just tear them up and dip them in the sauce.

TACO CHAFFLES

Serves: 2

Nutritional Information (per serving):
Calories: 258 | Carbohydrates: 4g | Fat: 19g | Protein: 18g

INGREDIENTS:

- 1 egg white
- 1/4 cup monterey Jack cheese, shredded
- 1/4 cup cheddar cheese, shredded
- 3/4 tsp water
- 1 tsp coconut flour
- 1/4 tsp baking powder
- 1/8 tsp chili powder
- Pinch of salt

DIRECTIONS:

1. Preheat the waffle maker.
2. Mix all the ingredients into a mixing bowl.
3. Divide the batter into two. Spoon the first half into the waffle maker and close the lid.
4. Allow the batter to cook for up to 4 minutes.
5. Remove the taco chaffle once cooked and set aside. Cook the remaining batter.
6. Using a muffin pan, set the taco chaffles between the cups, carefully molding it to form a shape similar to a taco shell.
7. Once the chaffles have set, scoop up some ready-made taco meat (or you can make your own) onto the chaffles. Allow to cool before serving.

CONCLUSION

I hope this book was able to help you along your keto journey. It's easy for anyone to be overwhelmed, especially when they're new to the ketogenic diet. This book has compiled a good number of recipes for one of the easiest keto-friendly foods—the chaffle.

If you have read and skimmed through this book already, the next step is to buy a waffle maker, and start gathering the ingredients you need for any recipe you wish to try.

I wish you luck in your keto journey!

Made in the USA
Columbia, SC
20 January 2020